Daily Reflections
For
Bar Exam Study

An Inspirational Companion
for Law Students and
Experienced Attorneys Taking
the Bar

M. G. Groepler

ISBN: 1441464115
EAN 13: 9781441464118

Printed in the USA

For Alex and My Fritz

"I am responsible for my own state of mind. I will not absorb any negativity or panic of others. Panic and clarity cannot coexist. Panic breeds panicked thinking. Calm and steadiness breed clarity of thought. I choose calmness and clarity."

\- M. G. Groepler

Introduction

This book is written with great compassion for you – the person who is preparing for any state bar exam — whether you are a first-time taker, a repeat taker, an attorney in another jurisdiction taking or re-taking another state's bar, or any combination of the above. Twice a year, thousands of law students as well as licensed attorneys sit for bar examinations all over this country. Attorneys taking the bar have an interesting challenge because they must, in effect, disregard how they practice law, and revert back to law school mode.

Though this book is for anyone taking any bar exam, it is *not* a substantive study guide of any kind. It was designed as a daily dose of positivity, a paper "pep talk" of sorts. Bar study can be tedious, tiring and stressful. Feel free to either read a page a day, read it all in one sitting, or just randomly open it anywhere when you need a break. *Regardless of the outcome of your exam, under no circumstance should any test result ever be confused with the measure of you as person or your identity.* Please remember this if ever things temporarily look a little bleak.

You are more than any exam. I wish you all great outcomes!

Acknowledgements

There are so many amazing people who have touched my life, and who by their very existence have had a butterfly effect on the creation of this book. The list is long, and to name names here will only serve to leave out many. I trust that those to whom I refer know their place in my life and their place in this little book. I am forever grateful for the blessings of those who I call family and dear friends. I would like to extend a very special thank you to my sister Rena Reese, the founder of www.soulsaloninternational.com, and a published author herself many times over. Rena, I thank you not only for editing this book, but for your words of persuasion, healing, and celebration that have always echoed in my spirit. I also thank my dear Mom and Dad, my brother John, and of course Jack, Meg and Kate. Last, I thank the love of my life — my Fritz — for your love. You all are the wonderful mosaic of my life.

—*Marietta Geckos Groepler*
www.peacockstrategies.com

Daily Reflections
for
Bar Exam Study

An Inspirational Companion
for Law Students and
Experienced Attorneys Taking
the Bar

M. G. Groepler

1.

Today before I dive into my planned study schedule, I will take a minute to focus on the fact that I am smart, that I have a law degree, and that I can do this, as many have before me. I will not let the fears and stresses of others derail my preparation.

People CHOOSE their approaches to challenges. I choose to work through all the material with a steady, planned pace, knowing I will be where I need to be on exam day. My plans include learning all the subjects required, taking the necessary practice tests, honestly tracking my progress, changing and adjusting course where needed, and maintaining a solid and singular focus on my goal. While I am following my plan, I will remember to take care of my body and mind. I will rest when I need to and eat sensibly when I should.

Knowledge and practice are critical – rest and calm are equally important. I commit to taking care of ALL of me – mind, body, and spirit.

2.

Today I will avoid the people and things that make me feel frenzied; I will calmly study what I need to study. I have all I require to do well during this preparation period. Though my study schedule may feel daunting at times, and the stack of workbooks and materials may appear intimidating, I will remember that I am one of many who will be successful in this endeavor. It can be done, and I will do it.

Slow and steady will be my approach. My study plan will be completed in a measured fashion. I am not expected to know it all at once. Layer by layer, page by page, hour by hour, and subject by subject, I will master the material.

Perfection is not the goal; significant, sustained, and accurate performance is. That, I can do. That, I will do. The word "doubt" does not exist for me.

3.

Today I will have a very specific plan regarding how I will spend my day; I will take it slowly and follow it methodically, and I will remain positive throughout this process. Sometimes I am not in the mood to be positive though – sometimes it seems like too much too fast. I will recognize and acknowledge these feelings. I know that I will feel this way at times – and that my frustrations are absolutely normal. On those days I will still push on – challenging myself with specific, tangible goals for the day, and then achieving those goals.

Before getting some rest tonight, I will reflect on the day, and be able to applaud my specific accomplishments. I accept that there is no mystery to thorough bar preparation – it is comprised of a string of productive days like this one, today. The simplicity of this statement is rivaled only by its accuracy.

4.

Today I will not make the mistake of considering a low score on a practice test as a negative, or as a wasted day. Rather I will acknowledge that learning comes through my daring to be tested, daring to see what I really know and what I really don't, daring to grade my own performance, and daring to look at the initial raw numbers.

Learning comes in stages and sometimes in clumps. Learning can also come in up and down spurts. I know this and accept this. Bar exam study is not a sprint – it is a mental and physical marathon. My run does not need to be flawless, but I do need to perform well and to finish the race, dotting the i's and crossing the t's as I go. I consider bar study as training of sorts – each day I am conditioning myself for the exam dates. Those dates are the ones that count. These days are the days that will get me there.

I intend to get there. And I will.

5.

Today I will acknowledge that if I am nervous about this exam, I will take 5 minutes, if I must, to worry about it. That's it – 5 minutes. I may even make a game of it. If I feel so inclined, I will look at a clock – and literally spend five minutes thinking about all the consequences of what could happen if the results do not go my way. I'll just get it all out of my system. Worry, worry, worry. When time's up, I will note that worrying did nothing for me. Then, it's back to the books. I will worry when and if I have something to worry about. Not before.

But before I get back to the books, I will take 5 more minutes, and just imagine complete success... getting the news that I have passed! I will think about who I will call... and how I will celebrate! I can see the party now!

6.

Today, for whatever time I have set aside, I will make a note to take a short break and do at least one fun thing – even if it is only a short call to a friend who always makes me feel great. This may seem like an odd thing to do in the middle of – oh, let's see – one of the most stressful events of my professional life!   But it is not strange at all.

The actual study, learning, memorizing, and practicing are only parts of what will make me a success on the exam days.   I need to show up rested and together on those days.   It will be easier to be calm and rested when it counts if I have accurately absorbed all the material studied, and articulated it to the examiner in a clear, cogent manner.

I have the skill and intellect to pass this test and the common sense to take care of myself while preparing for it.

7.

Today I will focus on having a very productive day. It will be easier to do this if I have been at my best when studying. Being at my best includes taking some time to relax, rest, email or call a friend or family member, or literally do anything that lifts my spirits and makes me laugh and smile. There is no harm in a fun mini-break! It may actually rejuvenate me and energize me so that I can dive back into the stacks of materials.

I understand that ironically, sometimes the very thing that will entice me to dive back into my routine, is actually a small respite from it. I will pay attention to my internal compass. If I need a break, I will take one. Even if I do not think I need a break, but I am feeling very tense or stressed, I will take one anyway. There is no shame in taking a breather. And I intend on making it a fun one.

8.

Today I will stay focused on my preparation. I will not allow panic, fear, and negative thoughts to control the energies of my mind. I will focus instead on absorbing the material and techniques that I need to be successful. I will take a fresh look at my study plan. Do I need more time with a daunting subject? Do I need more time with the multi-state practice questions? What about the essay portions and the performance test?

I will honestly assess these areas as well as my strengths and vulnerabilities. I will adjust my study time as needed to ensure that I have confidence in the areas that concern me – and that I maintain my strong performance in areas that come more easily to me.

9.

Today I will be open to the fact that I am identifying topic areas where I feel solid, and those where I feel less confident – so I can best assess what needs attention. My goal is not necessarily to feel carefree and super confident when I walk into the exam. While that may happen, it is not likely. (And probably not normal – anyone acting carefree may just be fooling themselves.)

Rather, I accept that no matter how hard I study, and how much I prepare, and how many practice tests I do, and even if I know I have a solid mastery of all the required areas, I know I will probably still be nervous. And that is NORMAL. Pretty much everyone is nervous.

I will not allow my nerves to distract me – no way.

10.

Today I will take a moment to absorb a simple truth. Although I have spent a great deal of time, money, and energy preparing for this test, I do not need to be "perfect" here! Though skill, knowledge and proficiency are important, I do not need to write the definite hornbook on contracts law! I need to have solid and accurate responses on all aspects of the test. No one is demanding a perfect exam from me; I only need a very solid exam – effectively covering the materials in the manner required by the graders.

I will study and practice the model answers, and I will adapt and conform to what is expected. I can do this.

11.

Today I will recognize the fact that others over the years who have passed this test are not any smarter than I am; they are simply people who have mastered the exam – not just the material, but literally mastered how to take and write the exam. Those people have also mastered themselves and their emotions for this challenge.

Their success has been due to a combination of the absorption of the materials, an understanding of how to effectively respond to the questions, and the choice to stay steady and rested. I can and will master those things too.

12.

Today, though I have every intention and ability to pass this examination, I will firmly acknowledge that this test is not a measure of me as a person; it is only a test. I need to be successful to move forward in my chosen field – yet I will constantly hold true to the fact that *I* am not this test. This test, or my performance on this exam, cannot dictate my identity. (I am more likely to forget this point, more than any other in this book.)

Yes, this is an important undertaking, but it does not define me. A positive result does not make me a better person – it will just make me a licensed lawyer. An unsuccessful result does not make me less of a person, it only means that the test requirements have yet to be mastered. No state board of bar examiners can ever measure my worth or value.

I can and will pass. No kidding. There is never an "if" – only a "when."

13.

Today I will acknowledge that it is OK to feel fear at times while studying for this exam – as long as I do not allow those moments to overpower me. Yes, it is an important test, but millions have passed it – and I can too. Sometimes I like to think of the staggering numbers of who have taken bar exams since way back. Thousands sit for each exam each July and February — so many have gone before me and done well. So many will be taking this exam long after it is a distant memory for me.

I will get through this studying, and get through the test. I, too, will be added to the lists of those who have passed. I can and will do this. For now, I resume my methodical, steady, and confident preparation.

14.

Today I will give this study process my best; I know that I must learn the black letter law as well as the exam techniques in layers. I cannot do it all in one day. One committed and productive study session after another wins the race. Sometimes it seems that the gradual studying is one of the hardest parts of this process, but that is how the most effective learning occurs. I will view each day as another brick in the foundation I am building.

Brick by brick, day by day, page by page – each day I am closer. I will remind myself that calmness, steadiness, and unwavering commitment to success will get me successfully through all facets of the exam. I will be patient, confident, and strong. I will not allow my occasional nervousness to derail me in any way.

Nerves at times are normal – especially as the test draws near. I can handle it. I will be steady, centered, and prepared on exam day.

15.

Today, though I may be feeling a little overwhelmed, I will not get bogged down by the seeming enormity of this task. I will be slow and resolute - as well as focused on my goal. I can do this. I will take a moment to reflect on some of the tough things I have experienced in my life – things that took patience, confidence, and perseverance. While this exam feels daunting, it is just a test. Yes, a big one – but just a test.

I refuse to get caught up in the drama of others I may see panicking as they prepare. I choose to not have any part of that reaction. There is no time, and there is no reason for drama. One day at a time – a trite saying, but very true.

That being said, I will do a great job today. I will be productive today. That's the plan.

16.

Today I will make sure I take a break. I will allow for time with friends or for something fun if time permits. If time feels very tight today, I will consider a short phone call to a good friend, a brisk walk, or even a few moments of relaxation listening to my favorite songs. I will not feel guilty about taking a little time away from my studies to do something that will raise me up, relax me, and make me smile. I know that a little respite will refresh me and give me renewed energy as I dive into my study materials again.

There's nothing wrong with a brief breather – after which I will pound those books, attack my outlines, be vigorous about necessary memorization, and tireless in my essay preparation. Bring it on; I am rested and ready.

17.

Today I will acknowledge that while preparation for this exam is critical, a calm, rested mind is paramount to success. If I am in a bar review class, I can see the stress that some students carry. It is clear that it can be contagious. I refuse to adopt the worries of others as my own. I am responsible for my own state of mind. I will not absorb any negativity or panic of others.

Panic and clarity cannot coexist.

Panic breeds panicked thinking. Calm and steadiness breed clarity of thought.

I choose calmness and clarity.

18.

Today I will remind myself of my many past accomplishments – I know I have what it takes to succeed at this. If I am a repeat taker, I will remember that I am in darn good company, and that I actually do have some advantages. I have endured the stress of exam conditions in the past. I have studied and already memorized a great deal. I have covered all the material in the past, and completed countless practice tests.

Now, I just need to assess, regroup, and use my past knowledge and experience to my advantage. I need to refine my technique and assess the areas which require more study.

I can pass this exam.

19.

Today I will take a moment and be thankful and grateful for the positive things in my life. I will actually take a moment to reflect on these things. Do I have a supportive family? Do I have good friends with whom I can freely talk? Do I have a decent place to study? What are the things in my life for which I am still very grateful? I will pause and mentally list these things.

I honestly do get some peace acknowledging the gifts in my life that make this process tolerable. After some reflection on this – to ground myself – I will turn to the task at hand – and do what must be done. I have what it takes to pass this. I have the intellect, calm, and perseverance to succeed.

Everything in my past has brought me to this point. I am ready.

20.

Today I will acknowledge that though I intend to pass this exam this next round, that might not happen. I will not focus on that, but I will acknowledge that such an initial result will not end my career.

Parts of me actually do not want to read this particular page – because I want to think only of success. So maybe I will skip this page. But if I need it, I will come back to it. Why? Because (of course), though I want only success, and I want it now – I need to be pragmatic.

On the small chance that I may need to repeat this test, I understand that I have the energy, stamina, and brain power to do so. So if I need to, I will re-tool and I will be back.

I will succeed. Period.

21.

Today, after my studying is complete, I will commit to getting to bed at a decent hour. I know I may have a tendency to stay up until all hours, or survive on coffee, but I need to make sure that I get adequate sleep.

Sometimes it is tempting to just keep on going through the wee hours of the night – and I admit that at times it does appear to pay off. There is a satisfaction in finishing whole sections of study and practice exams – and getting on a "roll" and plowing through. I cannot commit to never staying up late – because sometimes that does work best for me.

I am nonetheless accepting that the law of diminishing returns makes it clear that at a certain point, no amount of knowledge can replace good old-fashioned rest. (And that's especially true the night before the examination!)

22.

Today, even though I may be feeling sick and tired of this routine, I will remember that this process is finite, and that following a specific daily plan is all I really need. I may choose to methodically cross off the days of the calendar and keep a running list of all the material I have covered. This helps me track my progress and accomplishments. Having an inventory of where I have been and a plan for where I have yet to go is very grounding. Being grounded is very important. Why? Because when I am at the testing site with my laptop, or pens and paper, all that I have at that moment is the calm understanding that I have prepared, and that I am ready. My mindset is at that moment my most powerful weapon.

I acknowledge that my healthy mindset does not just appear the morning of the exam. The mindset is the product of my many previous days' work. It crescendos on test day. And when test day comes, I will be ready.

23.

Today I am going to take a minute vacation – I will close my eyes... and see it as clear as day... that day when I get my great news... that I passed! Whether I find out online, or by letter, I can envision the moment when I read my name coupled with the news of my success! As I receive the news, I will feel any worry and stress roll right off me. I will feel freedom and happiness! I am done! I have passed! No more testing! I did it!

I will hold this image and this thought in my mind, before turning back to the books. I know that this image of my passing – one I can see clearly – will be my reality.

That day will come. I will read my name and the news that I passed. I know that is what lies ahead. Success!

24.

Today is a new day of study and preparation. I have to admit that all these days are running together. Sometimes I am not sure what day it is. If I am studying full time, I often lose track of the hour. If I am working and studying, it can be a drain to balance all facets of my life.

Nonetheless, I am doing this. I am balancing it all. As the days behind me fade, the days before me stretch ahead. I will stay resolute, steady, and vigilant while managing my time. I will ensure that my time is spent wisely. I will not leave my studying to chance. Every day, I will have a plan. Every day, I am open and ready for more learning to take place – whether it be via more practice exams, memorizing, or essay writing.

I know I am getting closer to my goal with each day that passes.

25.

Today I know what I need to accomplish: I will proceed through my planned tasks, take a couple of breaks, and stay with it. I am fueled by the momentum of my progress. There are ups and downs, but I know that they are normal. This is a process that requires endurance. I am in this for the long haul, and I accept that my great return will come with slow and steady preparation.

This process cannot be rushed. I understand that success will come by doing just what I have been doing: slow and steady preparation. I know that my knowledge will increase each day as I absorb and master the necessary information. My confidence is also increasing daily, knowing that I am building the foundation of skills needed for success.

There are no shortcuts here – I must travel the entire road, and feel each step. Before I know it, I will look back and see the trail I have made. For now though, my focus is on moving forward.

26.

Today as I study, I will remain very focused. I will not entertain negative thoughts and worries, as they serve only to waste time. I will be objective as I evaluate how my study plan is working for me. If my plan needs to be updated, or needs an adjustment, then that's what I will do.

I will not make any changes out of fear; rather I will make them as affirmative refinements as to what I need to learn.

There is a difference between being strategic and being desperate. I choose to be strategic.

27.

Today I will evaluate my progress. I will give myself an honest assessment of my status. Understanding that a feeling of unease can go with the territory, I will not hesitate to refine my study plan, re-examine areas that require improvement, and take appropriate action.

Studying longer is not necessarily better than studying "smarter." I intend to do both: I will put in the hours needed, but I will be strategic as well.

I am going to pass this exam.

28.

Today I recognize that the test dates are getting closer, and while I am a little nervous, I can handle it. I am preparing diligently and seriously for the exams. I will credit the importance and power of the hours I have already put in. With each day that passes, I am that much closer to my goal. I know that it is normal to always wish for more time – I know I will make do with the time that is left.

I am on track for a successful result. I know test day will come and go – and after that, I look forward to a good rest!

For now, I will be diligent and steadfast. I have a study plan, and I will execute it. If I need to adjust it, I will. I am in control. I will succeed.

29.

Today I will consider whether I am taking care of myself. Am I too stressed to absorb any new information? Have I been eating healthy? Have I been sleeping? I will briefly take stock of my situation before hitting the books today. I will resist the urge to say, "I have too much to do! I will sleep in a few weeks! I will take some time for myself after the test!"

I acknowledge I need to be very diligent, aggressive and organized with my study. However, if I need some sleep, some food, or a little time away from the books, I will give myself what I need. If I rob myself of those basic things now, I may end up paying for it later, by running out of steam, harming my health, or shortchanging my optimum performance on the test days.

I commit to taking care of my basic needs while being extremely focused on my studies. I can and will do both of those things.

30.

Today I will not forget that while I have hours of study and preparation ahead, I still need to be fresh, rested, and thinking clearly to be successful. I will also pay careful attention to how I have chosen to manage my time for today. How am I splitting up my day? Is that working for me? Do I have a healthy balance between memorization and practice? Am I making necessary course corrections as exam day approaches? Am I paying attention to my state of mind, as well as my physical state?

I will find the balance between pushing hard toward my goal with great diligence and making sure that the engine that is my mind and body is cared for. In sports, effective performance on game day is never just about the plays that have been memorized – the state of the mind and the condition of the body also play a great role in the outcome.

I will tend to my body as well as my mind.

31.

Today I will visualize the day when these necessary preparations are behind me. Amidst all of these outlines, charts, books, and practice schedules, is my simple desire to master what needs to be absorbed, and to practice writing out responses consistent with past successful responses.

There is a fine line between the intense volume to be mastered and chaos. I choose order. There is much to cover – but I am up to the task. I have a plan, and I will execute it. I refuse to be intimidated by volume. I have been breaking this process down into its pieces, and that is working for me. While this is an all-consuming time for me now, I know it is temporary and it will pass.

I will move forward with what must be done, knowing that this is merely an important point in time – and not forever.

32.

Today I will take a moment to think of the people in my life with whom I interact as I go through this intense preparation time. Am I being a nightmare to be around? Am I appreciative of the nice things friends and family are doing to support me? Am I misdirecting stress at anyone who does not deserve it? Today I will take a minute to think of these people. While I do not have lots of extra time, today I will take some time to be grateful to those who are supporting me while I prepare. I might even apologize if I have been short with people who mean well. A phone call or email might be in order.

If I am just not up to that right now, I will say my thank-yous and apologies once the exams are done. I am lucky to have people in my life who wish me well. I need to believe in myself as much as they do!

33.

Today I admit I am getting weary of the repetition of this process. I know it is normal to feel this way. I am tired of these topics and all of this practice. The exam dates seem simultaneously too far away and too close!

I choose to take comfort in this repetition – it means I am building endurance for the long testing hours, and the material is flowing into me in a steady manner. I will not worry about how much more there is to master. I will stay on my schedule and believe in the process.

I am one of many who has gone through this. I can and will pass.

34.

Today, as I study, I will make a concerted effort to focus on positive as well as productive thoughts. I will eliminate negative factors as well as negative people and influences from my environment. I do not need to be in circumstances that are distracting or that drag me down.

I know different people handle this process in different ways, but I am not responsible for being a counselor to others who may be freaking out. I will find the balance between being kind, yet not getting drawn into other people's dramas. I will do what I need to do, study what I need to study, and be where I need to be to ensure a very productive day. That is my pledge to myself which will fuel my success.

35.

Today I will think about who or what raises me up. I will look at my schedule and insert a mini-break with someone special or enjoy an activity that does not interfere with my study plan, and that energizes me before I hit the books again. I will plan something in the near future that I can look forward to. Maybe I'll enjoy a quick coffee with a friend or family member after a bar review class or in between study blocks. Maybe I will carefully plan to see a movie after a good long day of studying.

I am not sure what I will choose, but I do commit to taking a little break to refuel, recharge, and realign.

36.

Today I am in the mood to push forward. The end is in sight! My goals are within reach! I have memorized, read, reread, written, and taken practice tests. I am in the groove. I know I can do this. I have been preparing. I know it is absolutely normal to wish there was more time – but everyone wishes for that.

How I decide to use my remaining time is almost as important as how much time actually remains.

I am ready to make good decisions regarding time management. I will continue to do my very best.

37.

Today is a new day. I will approach all I must do with a calm mind and a clear head. I will set my study plan for the day, and methodically implement it. If today is set aside to cover specific subjects, from soup to nuts, I will dive in. If today is a multi-state review day for me, I will study not only the questions that I answered incorrectly, but I will also review the answers and explanations for the responses that were correct – to make sure I am not skipping concepts I may have successfully guessed during practice tests. If today is an essay-writing practice day, then I will dive in as well.

Whatever my plan is for blocks of study time, I will move forward. There is only time for progress and pushing ahead. I will not get caught up wasting time and leaking precious energy on unproductive thoughts.

38.

Today, as I study, I will keep my positive focus on my goal. I know thousands have passed this exam over the years, just as I will. If there are outside influences that are not conducive to my preparations, I will do what I can to not be affected. If there are friends who are panicking, and need an ear, I will briefly offer an ear, say words of support, but then make it clear that worry cannot help us learn the material. Time, preparation, study, and practice are the tools for success. Though I do care about colleagues who may be having a hard time, I will kindly make the decisions that support them if I can, without jeopardizing what I must do.

People choose how to respond to stress. I choose to stay steady, focused, and calm.

I will not get caught up in the tidal waves of others.

39.

Today I will keep it simple. Study, eat, practice, memorize, short break, and then repeat and repeat and repeat! I will set a reasonable plan for what must be accomplished today and stick with it. Nothing grandiose or overly complex. I will create a simple doable plan for my intended accomplishments today and execute that plan.

Time management is as important as knowledge management. Knowledge management is as important as self-management.

I can do this. I am doing this.

40.

Today I will not be frustrated by those well-meaning folks who say, "Oh, OF COURSE you will pass!" They mean well, but they sometimes do not get it that such phrases can add pressure. I understand that they just do not know what to say, and want to say something. I will just say "thanks" and hit the books hard. I will not respond with energy-depleting phrases like, "Well, I hope so," or "Well, you never know...." I will not ever allow the confidence that others have in me to ever feel like pressure.

Pressure is an emotion that I can choose, or un-choose. I refuse to inflict pressure and stress on myself. Yes, this is serious business, but I will not lose sight of the fact that this is just a test.

I can and will keep my cool. I have everything I need to succeed.

41.

Today I will take a few minutes to assess how my study plan is coming along. Am I on schedule with what I need to be covering? Am I memorizing what I need to memorize? If I find that I need to make some corrections and adjustments, I will do so. However, I will make them in a strategic way.

I will NOT make changes out of fear or desperation. I accept that people studying for the bar virtually always feel that they need a few more weeks. I know that is normal. I will work within the time I have. I will work "smart." I can work smart because I AM smart.

This is just a test. A really important test, but a test nonetheless. I will never let it become a referendum on my value.

42.

Today I will think about success. That is my word for today. Success is about mastering the material, and revealing that mastery in a clear and acceptable manner to the grader. That's it. There are brilliant students and attorneys who also have to master the test and the content – that fact does not make them any less fabulous.

I may not feel fabulous at the moment, but I am. I will do what needs to be done to put this exam successfully behind me.

ONWARD.

43.

Today as I plan my day, I am actually filled with peace. That seems a bit odd, as I have this exam ahead of me, but I am filled with a calmness and a quiet peace.

I know that is because I have been studying. I have been practicing. I have been planning. I have been preparing. I have been taking care of my mind and my body. I have controlled all I can in this process. I am not perfect, but I am ready. I have prepared for quite some time now. I am actually getting to the point where I just want to take the test. I will maintain this feeling – this steadiness – through the whole exam process.

Peace is my mantra.

Serene is my state.

Tough is my mindset.

Optimistic is my outlook.

Success is my prize.

Notes

Notes

Notes

Notes

Notes

Please visit:

www.PEACOCKSTRATEGIES.com
to contact the author or to order
additional copies of this book. It
is also available on
www.amazon.com.

You can also visit
www.youtube.com under *"Daily
Reflections for Bar Exam Study,"*
for a companion video.

Made in the USA
San Bernardino, CA
09 May 2018